BEAUTIFUL WEDDING FLOWERS

MORE THAN 300 CORSAGES, BOUQUETS, AND CENTERPIECES

DIANE WAGNER

BEAUTIFUL WEDDING FLOWERS

MORE THAN 300 CORSAGES, BOUQUETS, AND CENTERPIECES

DIANE WAGNER

HEARST BOOKS
A division of Sterling Publishing Co., Inc.

New York / London
www.sterlingpublishing.com

Contents

1. Begin with the Flowers............. 7
   In Season • Color Palettes
   Sentimental Accents

2. Flowers for the Wedding Party ... 77
   Bouquets • Corsages & Boutonnieres
   For Flower Girls

3. Flowers for the Ceremony 113
   Down the Aisle
   Arches, Arbors & Chuppas

4. Flowers for the Reception 133
   Room Decor • Centerpieces
   Table Settings • Cakes

5. Making Floral Designs at Home....203
   Bouquets, Corsages & Boutonnieres
   Arrangements & Accessories

Photography Credits............... 221
Index 222

~ ONE ~
BEGIN WITH THE FLOWERS

Flowers are one of the most important elements for establishing the ambience of a wedding. The colors, textures, and style of the arrangements work together to create floral designs that will be admired and treasured the day of the wedding, and remembered forever after in photographs. The bride's choice of flowers reflects her personal style, and the colors, unique containers, and props selected all contribute to the finished effect. The possibilities are endless and enticing, so understanding the role flowers play in the festivities is key to narrowing the options and selecting the perfect floral decor.

Flowers adorn the bride, groom, and other members of the wedding party, the ceremony site and the reception venue; often they are chosen for a rehearsal dinner or other preliminary function as well. Which flowers are selected, and the way they are arranged, depends on personal taste; the season, the style of the venue, the size of the wedding, the overall formality or informality of the festivities, and the budget all affect this choice as well. You may be drawn to particular types of flowers, have a palette in mind, or want to base your decor on a seasonal or personal theme, and whichever approach you prefer will start you on the path to a beautiful, memorable day.

Let Mother Nature's bounty of seasonal flowers establish a theme for your wedding decor.

1. Spring flowers display some unique shapes that are not found at other times of the year: the delicate "bells" of lily of the valley, the ruffled cups of daffodils, and the tiny spears of grape hyacinth. Graceful lily of the valley makes a charming backdrop for these pretty pastel blooms.

2. At one time bridal flowers were traditionally white and ivory, but now brides frequently carry vivid colors and unusual flowers in their bouquets. These days, flowers are shipped all over the world, so you are often able to get flowers that are considered out of season, such as lilac in the winter and hyacinth in the fall.

3. The gentle colors of these blooms make this mix a perfect choice for spring celebrations. The round shapes of the pink ranunculus, soft coral poppies, and pink tulip contrast nicely with the tiny florets of fragrant lilac. Anemones, with their black centers, add a sophisticated touch, and the ruffled petals of lavender sweet peas provide a soft background.

4. Fresh, healthy blooms and interesting color schemes demonstrate a florist's attention to detail and love of flowers.

5. Spring flowers can be made to look delicate or contemporary by changing the arrangement and container style. These simple containers and single flower arrangements give a bold, modern look to springtime daffodils and hyacinth.

6. SPRING FLOWERS

At the first hint of warmth and sunshine after the long cold winter months, spring flowers offer bright, cheerful colors and delicate shapes.

- Daffodil
- Freesia
- Hyacinth
- Grape hyacinth
- Iris
- Lilac
- Lily of the valley
- Pansy
- Peony
- Ranunculus
- Tulip
- Violet
- Viburnum

7. A well-tended garden makes a lovely setting for a late spring or summer wedding or reception. Here pretty antique chairs are strategically placed so early-arriving guests can pause to enjoy the colors and fragrance of the peonies.

8. For the best value, use flowers that are in season and easily available. You will find a wide variety of flower types and a huge range of colors in every season.

9. This cheerful hand-tied bouquet is perfect for early spring. Bright yellow daffodils meld beautifully with pale peach roses and florets of fresh green viburnum. The stems are wrapped with yellow taffeta ribbon and "buttoned" with green pearl pins.

10. Gerbera daisies are not a common choice for wedding flowers but they add a lighthearted touch to a bridal bouquet. This informal example displays a glorious selection of vibrant summer flowers: hot pink gerbera daisies, delicate nerine lilies, mango calla lilies, yellow freesia, and green bupleurum.

11. Look to the garden when designing your bouquet. A florist can add a few stems of a sentimental homegrown favorite like yarrow, phlox, lilac, snapdragon, lamb's ears, or lady's mantle to the blooms he supplies.

12. SUMMER FLOWERS

Summer's warm temperatures and long growing season offer the widest choice of flowers, from dainty cornflowers to tall stalks of delphinium and foxglove. Take advantage of locally grown blooms for the best prices.

- BELLFLOWER
- CORNFLOWER
- COSMOS
- DELPHINIUM
- EREMURUS
- FOXGLOVE
- GODETIA
- LISIANTHUS
- PHLOX
- SCABIOSA
- STOCK
- SNAPDRAGON
- SWEET PEA
- VERONICA
- ZINNIA

13. Create a sunny theme for an informal summer wedding with a variety of daisy-type flowers. Traditional daisies are always fresh and lively with their yellow centers and white petals. Tiny Monte Casino asters resemble miniature daisies and add clouds of inexpensive soft fill in white, pink, or lavender. These pink coneflowers add another dimension to the daisy theme.

14. Bright pink star-shaped lilies look even more important when surrounded with soft green foliage and delicate flowers: choose fragrant lavender, long lasting statice, and interesting ferns.

15. Summer offers a glorious mix of bright garden flowers in various shapes, sizes, and colors. Arrange bright colors together as you see them grow in the garden.

16. Sweet pea is a beautiful bridal flower, available in white and shades of pink and lavender from pastels to deep violet. It is best suited to personal flowers or small arrangements in water. The delicate stems can be reinforced with fine wire for bouquets and corsages.

17. Place a vibrant garden bouquet in a simple, nicely shaped white jug for a bridesmaid's tea in the garden.

18. Roses, said to represent romantic love since Victorian times, are the sentimental favorite of most brides. On the practical side, they hold up extremely well. These classic beauties would be a beautiful addition to any bridal bouquet.

19. Candles work especially well in autumn themes, when the golden glow of candlelight complements the warm tones of fall flowers and foliage.

20. Dahlias offer a full palette of deep warm colors: coral, orange, red, burgundy, purple, and eggplant. The shape and texture of the full, multipetaled flower heads combine well with other late summer and autumn flowers.

21. AUTUMN FLOWERS
Autumn flowers present interesting textures and a rich, vivid palette of colors.

- AMARANTHUS
- ASTER
- CELOSIA
- COSMOS
- CROCOSMIA
- DAHLIA
- GOMPHRENA
- SOLIDAGO
- SUNFLOWER
- THISTLE
- HYPERICUM BERRIES

22. Add interesting blue thistle to traditional autumn flowers. The shades of blue-gray add a nice contrast to gold and orange flowers. An accent flower like thistle also makes a distinctive boutonniere, and when fresh it is very soft.

23. Twig, reed, or wood baskets add natural texture to floral arrangements, combining particularly well with the saturated warm tones of autumn dahlias.

24. SEASONAL BRANCHES
Add interesting branches to extend the height of large arrangements.

- SPRING: PUSSY WILLOW
- SUMMER: CURLY WILLOW
- FALL: OAK OR MAPLE LEAVES, RED BRANCHES
- WINTER: WHITE BIRCH

25. All lilies are very long-lasting—enjoy them for up to two weeks. As each open flower withers, remove it and the next bud will open. Every bud on the stem will open slowly, even the smallest one at the top. Because the flowers are large and so striking, even a single stem makes an impressive display. If you are arranging wedding flowers yourself, buy lilies five to seven days before so the flowers have time to open for the best display.

26. Carry classic velvety red roses for a Christmas-themed wedding. Unexpected accents of tiny pinecones add seasonal spirit as well as variety in color and texture.

27. Accent winter flowers like amaryllis, bouvardia, carnation, heather, protea, rose, and trachelium with soft seasonal greenery, such as pine and cedar.

28. WINTER FLOWERS

During the cold winter months a bunch of cut flowers or a small arrangement adds a touch of color and the promise of warmer weather. Enjoy long-lasting amaryllis and lilies as you watch each flower open. Star of Bethlehem develops into a cluster of tiny white flowers as each bud opens along the stem. Buy anemones tightly closed and watch the petals unfold, displaying a distinctive dark center.

- Amaryllis
- Anemone
- Cyclamen
- Euphorbia
- Ornamental kale
- Lilies
- Snowberry
- Star of Bethlehem
- Trachelium

29. An example of formal holiday decor, this creative tree-shaped arrangement combines beautiful gold ribbons with a variety of greenery, flowers, and fruit, anchored by a bed of mosses and trailing ivy. Open lilies add fragrance and color. The use of the usual holiday red is restrained, and the pink and deep burgundy of the flowers and fruit contribute to the overall sophistication of the design.

30. If you are planning a holiday wedding, check with the venue to see what decor will be in place. Clubs and restaurants often decorate lavishly, and those decorations can contribute greatly to the ambience of your event, at no additional cost to you.

31. For a winter wedding have bridesmaids carry pretty ivy wreaths embellished with a few red roses and ribbons as a change from the usual bouquet.

32. Dramatic lilies and soft lisianthus are two flowers that are available all year, in a wide variety of colors. When you need a large display for church flowers or an escort card table, lilies are a perfect choice for focal flowers. A single open lily flower in a small glass vase adds a pretty accent to cocktail tables or a powder room. The round lisianthus flowers combine beautifully with other bouquet flowers.

33. Don't be put off by the less-popular carnation. There are many beautiful varieties available. Consider small spray carnations with bicolored petals or striking deep-toned blooms with ruffled edges.

34. One of the least expensive and most long-lasting flowers, carnations can provide striking color and beautiful texture, especially if massed in monochromatic clusters when fully opened—this creates beautiful pavé-style centerpieces. Experiment with a mix of shades that complement each other and keep the arrangement low, simple, and very full. Using an abundance of any flower will make an impressive statement.

35. If your heart is set on roses but your wedding isn't planned for summer, you'll find florist's roses available year-round in a huge variety of sizes and colors.

36. Roses should be open to their peak of perfection for wedding bouquets and arrangements. The flowers will look their best when lush and full, making the most of each stem.

37. FLOWER CHOICES FOR ALL SEASONS

These popular wedding flowers are commonly available all year, in white, cream, and a huge variety of colors.

- ALSTROEMERIA
- ASTER
- CALLA LILY
- CARNATION
- CHRYSANTHEMUM
- CYMBIDIUM ORCHID
- DENDROBIUM ORCHID
- FREESIA
- GARDENIA
- GERBERA DAISY
- HYDRANGEA
- LILY
- LISIANTHUS
- NERINE LILY
- TULIP
- ROSE
- STOCK

You'll find flowers in nearly every hue—
use them to create or complement the palette
for your celebration.

38

38. Single-color bouquets of one flower intensify the shape and style of that flower as well as the color. Wispy ferns create a frame for this loosely structured bouquet of large open bluebird roses.

39. Single-color arrangements generally look more formal, especially when made with white, ivory, or pastel flowers. These elegant cream garden roses are beautifully displayed in a colored glass vase shaped like a classic urn.

40. FRAGRANT FLOWERS
It is best to use fragrant flowers in bouquets and corsages, where the person carrying or wearing them can appreciate their scent. Don't use heavily scented flowers near food.

- CASABLANCA LILY
- FREESIA
- GARDEN ROSE
- GARDENIA
- HYACINTH
- LILAC
- LILY OF THE VALLEY
- PEONY
- STARGAZER LILY
- STEPHANOTIS
- TUBEROSE

41. Experiment with strong color combinations like the pairing of cobalt blue on this decorative pedestal with a mass of deep pink roses.

42. Use different shades of one color to add interest to an all-rose bouquet. Here, traditional pale pink is combined with several shades of medium and vibrant pink.

43. NONFRAGRANT FLOWERS
These classics are commercially grown for florists and usually do not have a strong fragrance.

- ALSTROEMERIA
- ASTER
- CALLA LILY
- CYMBIDIUM ORCHID
- DENDROBIUM ORCHID
- GERBERA DAISY
- HYDRANGEA
- LISIANTHUS
- RANUNCULUS
- TULIP

44. Use a mix of warm and cool colors to suggest a country garden: coral spray roses, open pale yellow roses, pink lisianthus, blue delphinium, pale blue hydrangea, and purple veronica. The white bellflowers and tiny Monte Casino asters keep this arrangement bright and cheerful, adding variety with their unique shapes and sizes.

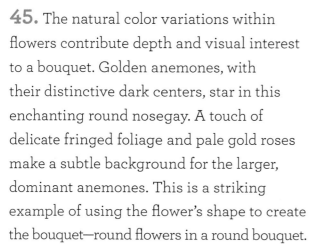

45. The natural color variations within flowers contribute depth and visual interest to a bouquet. Golden anemones, with their distinctive dark centers, star in this enchanting round nosegay. A touch of delicate fringed foliage and pale gold roses make a subtle background for the larger, dominant anemones. This is a striking example of using the flower's shape to create the bouquet—round flowers in a round bouquet.

46. An unexpected contrast, like this florist's display of cool violet and warm yellow, may spark your imagination to try new combinations.

47. Inexpensive glass vases in deep jewel-tone colors can enhance the color scheme. This cobalt blue bowl is a great choice to set off a loose arrangement of colorful summer flowers. To supplement the effect of a centerpiece like this, consider adding glass votives in the same deep blue color.

48. Vibrant red, coral, and pink blossoms look beautiful against assorted greens in this display of summer garden flowers. The variety of greens pictured here contributes to the natural quality of the display: Deep green leaves, fluffy light green viburnum, and for an unexpected touch, round balls of yellow-green brunia.

49. Roses and fresh mint, both straight from the garden, make a nostalgic centerpiece when casually arranged in an heirloom milk glass pedestal bowl. Just fill the bowl with water and place full blown roses in a compact, low cluster; then tuck in mint for a delicate accent. This is a lovely choice for a summer dessert table.

50. Tulips, daffodils, and roses create a cheerful bouquet with tones from pale to golden yellow that would be a perfect compliment to a soft green bridesmaid's dress.

51. Orchids are very long lasting, and these golden mokara beauties will stay fresh all day in a hand-tied bouquet. A single bloom can be delicately wired to create a matching boutonniere.

52. YELLOW FLOWERS

Add a ray of floral sunshine to your ceremony with these yellow blooms.

- Asiatic lily
- Calla lily
- Cymbidium orchid
- Dahlia
- Daffodil
- Freesia
- Kangaroo paws
- Mimosa
- Mokara orchid
- Oncidium orchid
- Poppy
- Ranunculus
- Rose
- Tulip

53. Orange is a lively choice for bridal flowers, particularly in the summer and fall. Shades range from pale golden orange to deep rust and always look beautiful against an ivory- or champagne-colored gown. This vibrant orange bouquet combines an exquisite selection of flowers at their peak bloom. The contrast of shades, textures, and shapes produces an interesting bouquet. The showy round roses and dahlias find their ideal counterpoint in the delicate petals of the Gloriosa lilies and orange asclepias, which are a perfect choice for soft, colorful fill.

54. The daffodil is one of the most charming and unusually shaped flowers. Available only in the spring, it is best suited to simple floral arrangements, which will show off its unique ruffled cup and surrounding petals.

55. Warm and cool colors always create a pleasing contrast. Classic blue-and-white pottery is a perfect companion to full-blown summer roses in delicate shades of peach and champagne.

56. This loosely gathered bouquet showcases a beautiful combination of spring flowers with a very feminine color scheme: blue-violet hydrangea is framed with lavender lilac and soft pink parrot tulips. Each flower introduces a distinctive color and texture.

57. Sweet peas in various shades of lavender clustered in small vases of similar hue make a soft, frilly, tone-on-tone accent to be placed on dining tables or grouped on a side table or mantel.

56

57

58. BEAUTIFUL BLUES Soft blue and purple shades that range from pale lavender to indigo and deep violet are found in many spring and summer flowers.

- ALLIUM
- CORNFLOWER
- DELPHINIUM
- HYACINTH

- LARKSPUR
- LILAC
- LISIANTHUS
- MONTE CASINO ASTER

- SWEET PEA
- TULIP
- TWEEDIA

59. Tiny florets of blue hydrangea are the perfect choice to display in a delicate hollowed out eggshell.

60. There are very few flowers that are truly blue. Delphinium is one, coming in a variety of blues from pale to intense that increases its appeal as a natural "something blue" for the bride. The long stems are perfect for large arrangements and florets can be individually wired to add to bouquets or boutonnieres.

61. This charming rustic basket is filled with clusters of tiny blooms perfect for the littlest flower girl. The combination of lavender lilac and pale green viburnum is freshened with a bit of white lilac. Even the beribboned basket handle is embellished with lilac florets.

62. Pale double tulips add just a hint of warmth and suggest the look of peonies at a fraction of the cost. Also, tulips are available early in spring, long before peonies. They look beautiful and graceful combined with other seasonal flowers.

63. Peonies are one of the most romantic, feminine flowers. Brides choose them for fragrance, color, and their beautiful shape. When fully open, the large flowers display multiple petals. The pink tones, ranging from very pale to intense fuchsia, are especially popular for June weddings.

64. THINK PINK

The palest pink will convey a romantic and traditional mood; shades of bright, hot pink impart a more contemporary feeling; and the deep pinks add warmth and look particularly dramatic in candlelight.

- Foxglove
- Hyacinth
- Peony
- Phlox
- Ranunculus
- Snapdragon
- Sweet pea
- Rose

65. The large, full flower heads of peonies add color, fragrance, and lushness. They are most often used for weddings in shades of pink or white, especially those with delicate burgundy veins at the center.

66. Pink is very popular for wedding flowers, and flattering to every complexion, and fortunately, every season offers flowers with a range of beautiful pink hues—roses like these with their pink-edged petals are only one example. This one color can be used to create many different moods by varying the shade, the type of flower, the container, and the design of the arrangement.

67. THE PALEST ROSES

Softly colored roses have become popular alternatives to pure white. Single-stemmed and spray roses are available in a range of subtle hues. Here is a list of some favorites:

SINGLE-STEMMED ROSES

- ANNA—THE PALEST HINT OF PINK
- CAMEL—WARM BEIGE
- PORCELINA—PINK/PEACH TONES
- SAHARA—SOFT SAND COLOR
- SANDY FEMA—HONEY-COLORED
- VERSILLA—PALE PEACH

SPRAY ROSES

- WHITE MAJOLICA—BARELY PINK
- CHAMPAGNE—VERY PALE PEACH
- ILSE—SOFT CORAL

68. Red adds warmth to autumn and winter arrangements. Cluster roses in a variety of shades from crimson to burgundy in bouquets and arrangements.

69. Don't get locked into the expected. An armful of bright red roses against a pure white gown makes a refreshing change from pastels for a June bride.

70. RED FLOWERS

Consider the following if you are looking for intense, vivid red blooms.

- AMARYLLIS
- CARNATION
- DAHLIA
- GERBERA DAISY
- GLORIOSA LILY
- HYPERICUM BERRIES
- JAMES STOREY ORCHID
- MOKARA ORCHID
- RANUNCULUS
- ROSE

71. To make an enticing first impression at the reception, arrange armloads of fresh red or hot pink garden roses in a large urn on the escort table to greet guests.

72. Rich red flowers enhance the warmth of candlelit decor. Each of these nosegays features the same flowers and colors, but in different combinations. The unstructured floral design is in counterpoint to the lineup of identical cream-colored containers.

73. Dark colors and unique blooms like the Hocus Pocus rose, in deep burgundy with delicate stripes of yellow on the velvety petals, are often used for dramatic contrast against a traditional white or cream bridal gown.

74. An arrangement with all-white blooms set off by green leaves always looks fresh and crisp. This appealing spring centerpiece features short pieces of flowering branches loosely arranged to cascade from a beautiful tall glass vase.

75. White flowers aren't always as delicate as they look. Some white blooms that hold up well in all weather conditions and during a full day of wedding festivities are roses, orchids, and calla lilies, making them excellent choices for both bouquets and decor arrangements.

76. Floating gardenias look glamorous and add beautiful fragrance. Center pretty bowls on cocktail tables and surround with votives for an easy centerpiece. Use a shallow dish for a contemporary look or a cut-crystal bowl for an elegant theme. Just remember that gardenia petals can turn brown when exposed to extremes of heat or cold, so handle carefully.

77. White flowers look especially fresh in the springtime with light green accents. Don't discard the pretty foliage from lily of the valley, hyacinths, and tulips. It can be used as an accent in bouquets and arrangements or to wrap the stems of flowers that are displayed in clear glass vases.

78. For chic country style, pair black and white anemones with a traditional pastoral French toile pattern—here updated in black and white on a porcelain pitcher.

79. WHITE FLOWERS

White, cream, and ivory are popular flower choices for a formal wedding at any time of the year. These are some of the most beloved traditional white flowers.

- CALLA LILY
- GARDENIA
- LILY OF THE VALLEY
- LILY
- ORCHID
- ROSE
- STEPHANOTIS
- STOCK

(81)

80. There is a current interest in green-colored flowers, from roses and orchids to hydrangea and pincushion protea. Green flowers can be used alone to create contemporary floral designs or paired with colorful flowers in place of foliage.

81. Shades of green look very fresh and contemporary, and a green bouquet will pop against a white gown. This hand-tied display features subtle shades of lisianthus with green dendrobium orchids and bright miniature chrysanthemums. The simple white satin stem wrap makes a very clean finish to the design.

82. GREEN FLOWERS

Flowers in shades of green used with decorative foliage create bouquets that are eye-catching and contemporary, and the color green signifies health and good fortune.

- AMARANTHUS
- ANTHURIUM
- BELLS OF IRELAND
- BUPLEURUM
- CELOSIA
- CHRYSANTHEMUM
- CYMBIDIUM ORCHID
- DENROBIUM ORCHID
- GREEN GODDESS CALLA LILY
- HYDRANGEA
- HYPERICUM BERRIES
- KANGAROO PAWS
- LISIANTHUS
- PINCUSHION PROTEA
- ROSE
- VIBURNUM

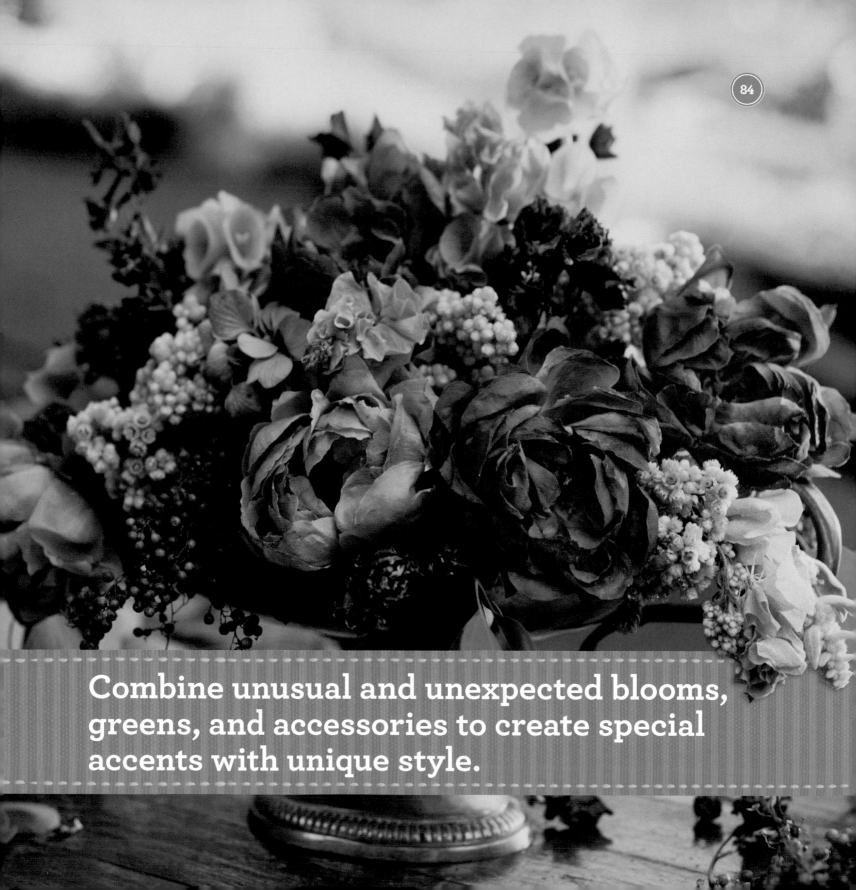

Combine unusual and unexpected blooms, greens, and accessories to create special accents with unique style.

83

83. Express your personal style with unexpected floral choices. In this bouquet a cluster of roses is surrounded with aromatic herb foliage, lavender, ferns, and trailing ivy.

84. The dense clusters of tiny pink pepper berry add complementary texture and color to this graceful arrangement, while a few stems of pale gray-blue-green, round-leaved eucalyptus drape delicately from the raised dish.

85. LAVENDER
It's pretty and fragrant, of course. Here are other reasons to include blooming lavender in your wedding.

- LAVENDER SIGNIFIES DEVOTION, MAKING IT A LOVELY AND SENTIMENTAL ADDITION TO A BRIDE'S BOUQUET.
- THE SOOTHING QUALITIES OF LAVENDER WILL CALM A BRIDE'S NERVES ON HER WEDDING DAY.
- LAVENDER'S RESTORATIVE QUALITIES ARE ALSO THOUGHT TO DISPEL HEADACHES.
- TO ENSURE TRANQUILITY BEFORE THE WEDDING, SLEEP IN LAVENDER-SCENTED SHEETS OR END THE DAY WITH A LAVENDER-SCENTED BATH.
- DRY SOME LAVENDER FROM THE BRIDAL BOUQUET TO MAKE A KEEPSAKE SACHET.

(86)

86. Curled fiddlehead ferns add a whimsical note to this classic arrangement of roses with trailing foliage. The footed compote provides just enough height to gracefully lift the flowers off the tabletop, showing them off to best advantage.

87. Enrich a bouquet or centerpiece with gilded ivy, which is a beautiful complement to flowers in warm hues at any time of the year and an elegant touch during the winter holiday season.

88. UNUSUAL ACCENTS

Sophisticated foliage and unusual natural materials add a touch of the unexpected to arrangements and provide a nice contrast when used with traditional bouquet flowers.

- Acorns
- Artichokes
- Bells of Ireland
- Fiddlehead ferns
- Feathers
- Lamb's ears leaves
- Lotus pods
- Ornamental kale
- Pomegranates
- Poppy pods
- Seashells
- Wheat and other grains

89. Lady apples, pears, cut limes, and a variety of berries enhance the attractive display of rich colors in this ceramic pot. The floral materials include pink and peach roses, burgundy miniature chrysanthemums, and deep-blue "antique" hydrangea, set off by glossy deep-green ivy leaves.

90. Herbs offer a delightful change from traditional foliage. Pretty yellow dill flowers add light, airy fill to the deep-toned carnations and roses in this winter nosegay.

90

91. HERBS A bride with culinary or gardening interests might want to consider adding herbs that have special significance to her bouquet and her groom's boutonniere.

- BASIL = GOOD WISHES
- CHAMOMILE = PATIENCE
- DILL = PROTECTION
- GINGER = STRENGTH

- MINT = VIRTUE
- ROSEMARY = REMEMBRANCE
- SAGE = LONG LIFE AND GOOD HEALTH
- VERBENA = SENSITIVITY

92. If you are looking to add an unusual floral detail, try kangaroo paw. It has a unique shape and good color range: yellow, green, orange, burgundy, and even black.

93. Lavender adds a refreshing accent of shape, color, and fragrance to bouquets. It is small enough to be wired into fragrant boutonnieres and corsages. If you have a garden, tuck a few homegrown sprigs into tussie-mussies for mothers to carry.

94. These reception dining tables are topped with contemporary square glass containers filled with hot red chili peppers that set off sleek white calla lilies. The use of rich red as an accent color is a beautiful contrast to crisp white linens. Simple place settings complement this casual yet distinctive decor.

95. Small floral arrangements or tiny vases with just a single stem gain importance when massed in a group. Together, the many shades of these pansies form a sea of purple on the tabletop.

96. Gather one flower type in a large vase for impact, such as these ruffled pink sweet peas, which create a soft cloud of color.

97. For the dramatic bride, this small bouquet displays a sophisticated mix of colors. The large lavender cattleya orchids and deep burgundy roses contrast vividly with the orange freesia. The choice of colors and minimal use of spiky foliage creates a very modern look.

98. The exotic pincushion protea adds texture and visual interest to this intriguing arrangement, where vibrant unusual flowers mix with some traditional choices. The large, spiky round heads of bright orange protea pair well with hot pink and coral dahlias, purple allium, orange Chinese lanterns, and interesting foliage. Stems of white pieris pick up the pattern color in the fabric table runner.

99. KEEPSAKE IDEA

Present flower-filled jewelry boxes to your bridesmaids. They will treasure the box long after the flowers have wilted. Scale the flowers to the size of the box and pick a different favorite color or flower for each attendant.

100. FLOWER MEANINGS

Many brides choose certain flowers for their traditional meanings. These are some wedding favorites.

- CALLA LILY = BEAUTY
- CAMELLIA = LOVELINESS
- CHRYSANTHEMUM = TRUTH
- FERN = FASCINATION
- HEATHER = ADMIRATION
- IVY = FIDELITY
- LILY OF THE VALLEY = HAPPINESS
- LISIANTHUS = APPRECIATION
- MYRTLE = LOVE
- PANSY = LOVING THOUGHTS
- ROSE = ROMANTIC LOVE
- ROSEMARY = REMEMBRANCE

101. Delphinium or hydrangea florets or rose petals frozen into ice cubes lend a romantic note to summer drinks. Offer guests iced sparkling water or lemonade as they arrive for a garden ceremony. Just make sure that all flowers used near or with food are grown without chemical pesticides.

102. Freeze ferns and flowers into ice surrounding bottles of white wine and vodka for the cocktail hour.

103. Adhere ferns to 2- or 3-inch diameter ivory pillar candles to create one-of-a-kind candles with a delicate springtime look. This can be done well in advance (see page 217 for directions). It is an attractive detail for the cocktail hour, and an effective way to cut down on your floral budget.

104. Delicious handmade chocolates are always enjoyable gifts. These are packed in shiny silver boxes tied to resemble the tiers of a wedding cake, with a sprig of berried eucalyptus to top off the bow.

105. Find a baker who will ice heart-shaped cookies to match your floral theme and add special sentiments. These artfully designed cookies demonstrate great skill and a steady hand.

106. Pack decorated cookies or special candies in small white boxes or cellophane bags tied with pretty ribbons colored to match your flowers as thoughtful favors for your guests.

~ Two ~
Flowers for the Wedding Party

Personal flowers—those carried or worn by the bride and groom and their attendants—are usually the first items of the wedding's floral decor to receive attention. Often the bride has been dreaming of her bouquet for years, and may have definite ideas about the flowers she wants to carry. Bridal bouquets can be large or small, sophisticated or simple, filled with glorious colors or subtle shades of pinks or cream. Whatever the bride's choices of individual flowers, they should be of impeccable quality and the bouquet designed to complement her gown, figure, and personality.

The selection of all other personal flowers will be determined by the bride's choice of what she will carry. Bouquets for the bride's attendants may echo or contrast the bridal bouquet. Corsages are typically selected for mothers of the bride and groom, grandmothers, and other female relatives. The groom, best man, groomsmen, ring bearer, fathers, grandfathers, and other male relatives wear boutonnieres. Flower girls may carry baskets, pomanders, or nosegays, and often wear floral headpieces or have floral embellishments on their dresses. Special friends or relatives who have a part in the wedding ceremony or are helping with the details of the day are also typically honored with fresh flowers.

Be true to your dreams when you select the bouquets for yourself and your attendants.

(107)

(108)

107. This classic hand-tied round bouquet features a nostalgic combination of colors and spring flowers. The shades of lavender and blue from the fragrant hyacinth and lilac, as well as the grape hyacinth, make a lovely contrast to the pink roses and tulips.

108. Bright clusters of Sweet William complement open roses in this informal, colorful bouquet.

109. Larkspur and dendrobium orchids are good choices to add length to a bouquet. Naturally long-stemmed, they don't need supplemental stem extensions.

110

110. Calla lilies are an excellent choice for a long-lasting bouquet. They can be combined with other flowers or used alone for a sleek, elegant look. The unique shape of the flower creates a lively sense of movement within the bouquet.

111. Glossy deep-green leaves emphasize the creamy tones of these soft, open roses. A casually gathered and tied bouquet like this is ideal for an informal celebration at home or in a garden.

- **HAND-TIED:** Flowers with strong stems, such as roses, are the best choice for round, hand-tied bouquets.
- **WIRED:** Small or delicate flowers with thin stems need to be wired for support. Cascading bouquets make use of wiring techniques to extend the length of stems and enable the flowers to move gently.
- **FLORAL FOAM BOUQUET HOLDERS:** Foam bouquet holders should be used if the weather is very warm or if flowers need to stay fresh for a long period of time. The floral foam is usually soaked in water with floral preservative to extend the life of the bouquet.

113. Long, flowing cascade-style bouquets often rely on hand-wired flowers to create the length. This is the most labor-intensive method of making a bouquet. Stephanotis, orchids, and gardenias all must be hand-wired for use in bouquets.

114. Choose fully open roses for a loose presentation-style summer bouquet, in which the flowers are tied with the longest stems on the bottom. Here pale lisianthus blooms frame the roses while fuchsia-hued astilbe and a few ranunculus add deep color and textural contrast. This timeless bouquet is finished with a collar of airy white Queen Anne's lace.

115. Bouquets that are made in foam bouquet holders are often thought to look rigid, but in the hands of an experienced wedding florist that won't happen. This lavish bouquet demonstrates the skill needed to make a natural-looking display. It will last from a morning ceremony until late in the evening.

116. Cascading bouquets can be scaled up or down, but as a general rule the larger and longer bouquets are most attractive carried by taller brides.

(118)

117. Tying small flowers, buds, ivy, and leaves to the ribbon streamers of a bouquet is a custom that began with the Victorians.

118. The color blue is said to bring good fortune to brides. Make your "something blue" a few light blue blooms added to your bouquet. This very romantic bouquet is made of cream roses with accents of soft blue hydrangea florets and white dendrobium orchids. The pink roses add an ultra-feminine touch.

119. KEEPSAKE IDEA

There are companies that will professionally preserve your bouquet. Make all necessary arrangements in advance, as the bouquet will need to be packed and shipped immediately after the wedding.

120. This keepsake quality floral crown is handmade of dainty cream silk roses with a border of pearls.

121. Have your florist make a headpiece of wired flowers that can be curved to suit your hairstyle. Order a simple veil on a comb to sit under the flowers.

122. Silk flowers are another good choice for brides. This charming bridal headpiece is fashioned from pastel silk roses. It is comfortably lightweight and easy to wear throughout a day of festivities, and the veil detaches for dancing.

123. Silk flowers for a headpiece should be carefully chosen to coordinate with the fresh flowers chosen for the bouquet. For a pretty effect, scatter delicate silk petals or small florets at the edge of a train-length veil to float down the aisle with the bride.

124. The generous size of these golden roses makes them a perfect choice for a large hand-tied bouquet. Scabious provides accents of deep burgundy and veronica adds interest to round-shaped flowers with a few graceful trails of purple. Spray roses and coral lisianthus fill the spaces between the large roses, creating a beautifully rounded shape.

125. Small or more expensive flowers such as miniature calla lilies, lady's slipper orchids, stephanotis, and sweet peas, which might not be fully appreciated in large decor designs, add exquisite detail to bouquets. This traditional all-white bridal nosegay combines fragrant stephanotis and gardenias with roses.

126. Jewels can be used to dress up a bouquet: center a crystal pin in each rose or scatter delicate sprays of crystals between the flowers. Use faux diamond-headed pins to detail the handle wrap, or thread ribbon through a jeweled buckle. A favorite heirloom brooch can be pinned to the ribbons as a sentimental "something old."

127. These large pale peach roses are gathered into a structured nosegay with lavender caspia to soften the round shape, and pink miniature carnations to add depth.

128. A bouquet of roses of the palest hues, accented with traditional stephanotis and lilies of the valley, looks beautiful framed with delicate lace.

129. KEEPSAKE IDEA

After the ceremony, send your flowers to a professional to have them waxed. This invitation, framed by bits of lace and a graceful arc of waxed roses, is a beautiful way to preserve your wedding memories.

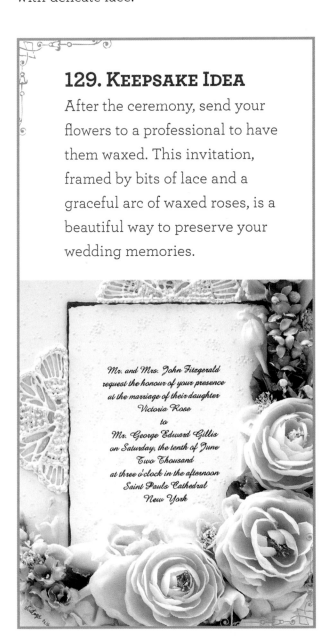

Mr. and Mrs. John Fitzgerald
request the honour of your presence
at the marriage of their daughter
Victoria Rose
to
Mr. George Edward Gillis
on Saturday, the tenth of June
Two Thousand
at three o'clock in the afternoon
Saint Pauls Cathedral
New York

130. Hand-tied bouquets will be at their freshest if kept in water until needed. Add ribbons at the last minute and trim the wet ends of the stems.

131. A petite bride should keep her bouquet to a small scale so as not to overpower her figure. If using large flowers, just a few well-chosen blooms of impeccable quality make an effective statement.

132. Berries are usually thought of as an accent for fall flowers, but hypericum berries are available in a range of colors that make them perfect for use all year. Peach hypericum berries match the roses in this informal bouquet, but the berries are also available in cream, golden yellow, green, bright red, and burgundy.

132

133

133. For an unexpected twist on the usual, have attendants carry pale bouquets while the bride carries brightly colored flowers like these vibrant orange roses.

134. Don't be afraid to mix colors and textures: bright green hypericum berries are a lighthearted accent in this bouquet of soft peach roses, coral miniature calla lilies, and cymbidium orchids. Orchids are available in a huge range of colors and interesting shapes that combine attractively with many other flowers.

135. Keepsake Idea
This romantic heart-shaped wreath features dried flowers from the bride's bouquet and the French braided lace used to wrap the original bouquet stems.

137. Keepsake Idea

Capture the sentiments of the occasion by embellishing one of your wedding shoes with an assortment of waxed flowers from your bouquet.

136. Keepsake Idea

Fill tiny terra-cotta flowerpots, silver julep cups, or mossy baskets with dried bridal roses or peonies. If you aren't able to dry the entire bouquet, this is a very pretty way to save one or two perfect blooms.

138. Add plenty of streamers to the bride's tossing bouquet: narrow satin or shimmery sheer organza will give kite-tail movement to the toss.

139. If the bouquet is bright and multicolored, keep the ribbons neutral. Green is always a good choice. Pick a soft shade of celadon, moss, or sage to complement the flowers. These cheerful bridesmaids' bouquets are tied with light green organza ribbon, setting off the warm pink and coral tones of the flowers. The florist has attractively displayed the bridal party's flowers with the bouquets in water until the last minute to ensure freshness.

140. This pastel bridesmaid's bouquet is beautifully framed against a classic black dress, an elegant mix of sweetness and sophistication.

141. Attendants' flowers will be much more interesting if the same blooms are used in each bouquet but in slightly different combinations. This will prevent the cookie cutter look in photographs.

142. Bouquets should complement or contrast with the attendants' gowns, not match them. These classic bridesmaids' nosegays of coral and cream roses would look stunning with celadon or moss green dresses. They are beautifully finished with wide organza ribbon and a satin stem wrap.

143. This pair of pretty bouquets presents a surprise of light-green poppy pods and soft lamb's ears leaves nested among open pink and white roses, freesia, and hydrangea.

144. Headpieces for attendants are no longer in fashion but a single blossom from the bouquet, such as a rose or a gardenia, makes a pretty hair accessory, especially if the attendants wear their hair up.

143

Corsages and boutonnieres add a small but delightful and elegant flourish to their wearers' attire.

145. Pin-on corsages, the customary mother-of-the-bride flowers, are best used if she is wearing a suit or dress and jacket.

146. Pale shades like champagne and blush are good neutral choices for mother-of-the-bride flowers; use them instead of trying to match her dress color.

147. Careful wiring of the flowers will ensure a corsage is as lightweight as possible.

148. As an alternative to a corsage, a floral spray can be designed to pin onto a small fabric handbag. Wrist corsages are a must for strapless dresses or delicate fabrics. They are also less likely to become crushed when dancing.

150

149. A small posy is a nice option for mothers. Many women prefer to carry their flowers rather than wear them. The mother's nosegay could include a few of the bride's flowers for sentiment.

150. Use flowers with thin stems, such as sweet pea and spray roses, in bouquets made for tussie mussie holders. Bulky stems will not fit the narrow opening. However, the stems of diminutive bouquets may be wrapped with ribbon as an alternative to a holder.

151. This beautiful collection of tussie mussie holders is from the Smithsonian Institution. You may be lucky enough to have one as a family heirloom or to locate one in an antiques shop. Many companies make reproductions, available at all price levels.

152. If your groom is the type who rebels at wearing fragrant flowers, give him a sleek single white miniature calla lily or a cymbidium orchid. These boutonnieres back white calla lilies with rose foliage. The groom's boutonniere is accented with stephanotis to match the bride's bouquet. The decorative tendril at the end of the stem echoes the curved tip of the calla lily.

153. A classic rose boutonniere can be individualized in many ways: accented with ivy and berries, fanned with leaves, or set against a folded single leaf. The stems can be simply clipped and wrapped with corsage tape or ribbon, curled into a tendril, or twisted with copper wire.

154. An all-white boutonniere will sparkle against a dark tuxedo. Add elegance with a silver ribbon instead of the usual green stem wrap. Grooms often wear white roses, but it is a sentimental tradition to use a flower from the bride's bouquet for the groom's boutonniere.

155. Boutonnieres for best man and groomsmen should match the attendants' bouquets. If using a mixture of flowers, pick the one best suited to boutonniere use.

156. Boutonnieres for fathers should coordinate with the mothers' flowers. Neutral colors or a paler version of the attendants' flowers are nice choices.

157. A boutonniere with unusual touches is a fun alternative, especially for the groom who shies away from wearing traditional flowers. Try small green Kermit mums, a touch of colorful celosia to accent a lisianthus bloom, or bright variegated leaves to back a cymbidium orchid. For a dressy holiday theme, back spray roses with a gilded ivy leaf.

Choose the sweetest, most adorable baskets, nosegays, and accessories for your flower girls.

158. Fresh spring flowers adorn these beautifully detailed baskets: Soft pink roses hold a cluster of lily of the valley and the basket of lilac has a dainty trimmed handle. A flower-decorated basket is a good choice for the flower girl to carry if your wedding site does not allow tossed petals.

159. Give your flower girl a ribbon-bedecked basket trimmed to match the attendants' dresses.

160. Fashion a floral garland for two children to carry as they walk down the aisle together. Having a partner can calm wedding jitters for young first-timers.

161. High-quality silk flowers are perfect for young flower girls: They look beautiful, become lasting keepsakes, and are practically indestructible! This lovely selection pairs pastel silk flowers with specially selected ribbons to make a dainty halo, a pretty pink and ivory pomander, and a barrette with a cluster of rosebuds.

162. These dainty flower girl nosegays have plenty of ribbon streamers that dangle in front of the little girls as they walk down the aisle. Young girls love colorful flowers, and a smaller variation of the bridesmaids' bouquets will delight them.

163. Little girls look adorable carrying round floral pomanders, which are suspended from a ribbon handle, making them easy for young children to hold. Use sturdy flowers, such as miniature carnations, small roses, or daisies.

164. Simple dresses look so sweet on very young flower girls. White cotton smocked dresses are summer classics and make a lovely background for the girls' flowers.

165. Add antique floral buttons to embellish a white or pastel-colored flower girl's dress. Choose sweet buttons that match the theme or colors of the wedding flowers.

166. Make a custom sash for your flower girl by sewing silk petals to a length of ribbon. Or pin a large silk blossom to the back of the flower girl's dress as a special detail for all to appreciate as she walks down the aisle.

This is just to say "Good-Morning,
As we each go on our way;
May the glory of the Morning
Stay with you all the day."

A Happy Easter

Handpainted Porcelain
Button Sets
Porcelain Rose Signal Hill CA

Handpainted Porcelain
Button Sets
Porcelain Rose Signal Hill CA

~ THREE ~
FLOWERS FOR THE CEREMONY

Wedding ceremonies today can be as lavish or simple as desired. When choosing floral designs for the ceremony venue, remember that these arrangements will be the first ones your guests see. They can set the style for the rest of the wedding decor or make a dramatic contrast to what will be seen at the reception. The type of ceremony you plan will determine the style and quantity of flowers needed to complete your vision. Many brides prefer to keep ceremony flowers to a minimum and focus more on decor at the reception location, where guests will spend most of their time. After all, during the ceremony the bride and groom will be the center of attention.

It's lovely to welcome guests and signal the occasion of a wedding to passersby by placing flowers on the exterior of the church or other venue. Wreaths on the doors, trim for stair railings, urns or large arrangements on steps or porches are some choices. Inside, flower-filled urns or baskets, a flower-trimmed unity candle, or other arrangements for the altar are typical. To frame the bride's walk down the aisle, consider candle stands, pew bouquets, or petals on the walkway. If there is an arch or chuppa, decorate it with blooms that match the wedding theme.

Adorn the vestibule and aisle with floral accents that lead all eyes to the bride.

167. Large floral arrangements in a foyer or vestibule create a welcoming ambience. For a ceremony in late winter through spring, take advantage of flowering branches, which look lovely massed in large urns. White apple blossoms or soft pink cherry blossoms are traditional for weddings. Coral-colored quince is beautiful but watch for thorns. Other choices are magnolia (pink), dogwood (pink or white), pussy willow, and bright yellow forsythia.

168. Cone flower holders are very pretty details that can be functional as well as decorative and are found in all areas of wedding decor: decorating doors and aisle for the ceremony, and later for centerpieces and favors at the reception.

169. If there are steps leading to the church or ceremony site, embellish the railing with garlands and trailing ribbons to match the colors of the flowers used inside.

168

170. This personalized aisle runner provides the finishing touch to an extravagant ceremony decor. Tall gold candelabra hold magnificent floral arrangements and clouds of petals blend the straight edges of the runner into the dark carpet.

171. A custom aisle runner may feature a meaningful quote hand painted amidst a floral pattern. One like this is an investment that is often passed from one family member to another.

172. Monograms are another option for a custom aisle runner; this one is set against a stylized floral pattern reminiscent of a damask fabric.

173. EXPERT ADVICE:

If you are having a runner custom-made, take a cue from Julie Goldman, owner of The Original Runner Company and creator of the runners shown here, who often takes inspiration from the wedding flowers when designing the colors and motifs on her one-of-a-kind aisle runners.

174. If the ceremony is held outdoors, discourage guests from walking on the aisle by tying a ribbon across the end. This will guide them to take their seats from the sides, keeping the center aisle fresh for the wedding party.

175. For a ceremony performed in a garden, use a profusion of petals to define the bridal aisle.

176. If you're looking for flowers to take apart so you can scatter their petals, roses and carnations are good choices; they both are multipetaled and available in a wide range of colors. Ask for soft, open roses slightly past their prime because these are easier to pull apart. You don't need top-quality petals to scatter along an aisle, as they will be quickly crushed by the bridal party's footsteps.

177. Aisle bouquets are usually positioned on every other chair or just the first few rows or pews. They add a great deal of impact, and a very personal touch, by bringing the flowers directly to the guests' view. These flowing red bouquets are designed with delicate curving stems that lead the eye to the matching petals on the grass.

178. Use ribbons to hang cones on the backs of chairs or on church pews in place of the usual ribbon or tulle bows.

179. With their whimsical shape, cones are charming holders for aisle nosegays. Metal cones can be displayed on stands placed directly in the grass.

180. This hanging bouquet would be equally at home marking the end of the aisle or on the backs of the bride's and groom's chairs at the sweetheart table. If the ceremony and reception are at the same venue the pieces can easily be moved.

181. These rented gold ballroom chairs are trimmed with fully opened peonies. If you wish, after the ceremony, while guests are busy during the cocktail hour, the chairs may be discreetly moved into the dining room, with the flowers still in place.

182. At once elegant and simple, hand-tied bouquets of long-stemmed deep orange roses add a pretty flourish to classic gold ballroom chairs. Generously positioned as these are on every chair lining the aisle, they create a beautiful frame for the bride's walk to the altar.

183. Aisle bouquets are one of the easiest ways to add color and detail to the ceremony. They can be made of any flowers, in any size, and are much more economical ceremony decor than larger arrangements.

184. Hang dazzling red pomanders from chairs along the bridal aisle. These are made of silk roses, which allows for an early setup. The dark wood chairs they adorn are reminiscent of church pews and create a warm, inviting setting for an intimate ceremony.

185. Place tossing petals in charming baskets like these, which are trimmed with green cymbidium orchids, graceful white freesia, and celadon green ribbon.

186. Fresh petals can be prepared the day before the wedding. Top them with damp tissue paper to keep them fresh overnight, and store them in a cool spot. Before the wedding ceremony, transfer the petals to pretty decorated baskets and offer them to guests.

187. Dried petals for tossing at the newlyweds can be prepared well in advance of the wedding. Gather friends to help you tie petals into squares of tulle or small organza bags. Arrange the packets in a pretty basket and designate a special friend to pass out the bags to guests as they enter the ceremony area.

Provide a lovely setting for the ceremony with a romantic floral arch or arbor.

188. Make use of a natural focal point when staging an outdoor wedding. This unforgettable scene features a floral arbor at the base of a massive tree.

189. A pretty chapel in a rustic setting needs very little in the way of floral decorations. The traditional white flowers in the garland and urns match the white chair covers, contrasting nicely with the leafy surroundings.

190. Simple garden arches can also be decorated to make a charming but less costly statement. Cover an iron or wooden arch with ivy, vines, fresh nosegays, or flowering branches in the springtime, to form a beautiful frame for the bride, groom, and officiate.

191. This existing structure on a beach is embellished with a traditional arch of greens and flowers to create a more intimate setting for the ceremony. The scenery is so dramatic that a simple decor is best, so only minimal flowers are used on the chairs and aisle stands. The warm colors of the flowers coordinate with the soft chiffon ties on the chairs and aisle stands, blending beautifully into the exotic locale.

192. This chuppah is made from thick, fresh green bamboo. Smilax vines soften the corners and bright flowers contrast with the neutral tones of the rocky coastline. The chuppah is set directly into the sand, with the rolling waves providing a dramatic background.

193. Outdoor wedding arbors and chuppas can be designed to blend into or contrast with the surroundings. For a rustic look, white birch support poles can be twined with grapevines, covered with moss and roses, or gracefully draped with billowing chiffon.

~ Four ~
Flowers for the Reception

A wedding reception is the time when family and friends join the celebration as participants rather than witnesses. The decor of the reception hall should be festive and express the taste of the bridal couple. From a lavish welcoming urn of spectacular seasonal flowers to an individual rose on each napkin, attention to details shows your guests that they are attending a very special event and how much their presence means to you. If your celebration includes a rehearsal dinner, cocktail party, breakfast, or similar event as well, take the same care with flowers and accessories for it.

As you plan the flowers and table settings, take into account the architecture and existing decor at the site to make sure your choices enhance rather than clash with it. Many ballrooms have neutral wall coverings, draperies, and chair upholstery, but if you do choose a site with a distinctive style or color, work with that decor to ensure the most beautiful ambience for your wedding. Or for an outdoor reception, take advantage of garden features and views to site a tent or decorate a terrace. When placing flowers in a room make use of existing architectural or landscape details to create focal points. If you wish, allow your and your fiancé's shared interest to take pride of place for the decor and choose a theme that reflects some passion, for instance, love of wine, or the beach.

Use beautiful floral arrangements to create a welcoming, memorable ambience in your reception hall.

194

194. This opulent design set in a lovely white tent offers flowers and candlelight at every level, creating a balance from table to table. Two high centerpieces of different styles have equally strong visual impact, are complementary, and add variety. Candelabra with fluted hurricanes are wreathed at the base by a generous display of cream flowers. The tall floral centerpieces are set atop narrow silver fluted vases, and accented with low candles.

195. Here a classic blue-and-white palette, embroidered table linens, and vintage crystal set the scene for an exquisitely designed dining table. All the tabletop items, including the flowers, are scaled to fit the round table. Everything harmonizes so well that the overall effect has more impact than any one element.

196. All the elements of the decor work together to create this inviting setting. The room lighting is carefully coordinated to the warm colors of the flowers, setting a very festive mood. The clean lines of the white paneled walls and mirrors complement the sleek floral styling, and the purple and green table arrangements are fresh and contemporary against the white linens and black chairs.

197. A rustic inn with a warm, cozy ambience is the perfect venue for a small, intimate wedding. Here the warm tones of the wooden beams contrast with beautiful champagne-colored table linens, and an eclectic selection of chairs completes the very personal decor. Guests will feel comfortable at the small tables, designed to encourage conversation.

198. If the room decor is formal—think swagged draperies and crystal chandeliers— stay with that theme. This is the place to use ornate floral containers, candelabras, and an abundance of flowers and candles.

(199)

199. For this Christmas wedding, pine trees ring the dining room and garlands and wreaths trim the windows to create a total holiday environment.

200. A tiered chandelier festooned with berried holly hangs above colorful poinsettia plants, forming a magnificent "tree" that welcomes guests at the escort-card table of a Christmas wedding.

201. Because the room decor tends to be so abundant at Christmastime, you can keep table decorations to a minimum. Use a profusion of candles to intensify the glow of the tiny Christmas lights. Choose gold ballroom chairs and opulent table linens to enhance the holiday cheer.

202. Because guests will be at the reception for several hours, including sitting at a table during the meal, floral decor is very important to creating ambience. Use the largest part of your floral budget to set the mood and make an impact where it will be most appreciated.

203. There are ways to use candlelight to suit every decor and budget: elegant candelabra, simple glass votives, bright pillar candles, traditional tapers, hurricanes, luminarias, and floating candles. Here beeswax tapers in antique candlesticks shed a warm glow. Just remember, candles should only be used at sunset or later, never early in the day.

204. The banister in this reception hall is ready for the bride's entrance down the staircase. A cloud of gold wired ribbons tops a cascading arrangement of seasonal greens, bridal white roses, and lilies. The small fruit and pink roses pick up the decorating details from the tabletop arrangement.

205. The softly draped fabric flowing down the center of this striking poolside table evokes the nearby water, while the rose petals scattered on the fabric replicate the flowers floating in the pool.

206. Visual interest at every level, from pleated fans to the vivid mix of low flowers, and the light, airy orchids floating in a graceful canopy above tall slender vases, make this colorful table an eye-popping, dramatic success.

207. EXPERT ADVICE:

Custom-made table linens can enhance your venue's existing decor or turn a simple party space into an unforgettable environment. Ann Davis, owner of the Total Table, in Philadelphia, emphasizes that floral choices should have a direct influence on linen selection. She suggests choosing fabrics that echo the color of your flowers if you wish to make a dramatic statement with color, or using linens in a single contrasting hue to set off the colors of your blooms.

206

208. Fabric chair covers are an inexpensive rental item, designed to fit on standard ballroom chairs, and can be ordered to match or contrast with the table linens. These white covers hide unattractive chairs that would detract from the pretty color scheme of the table centerpieces.

209. This one-of-a-kind table ensemble grabs the eye with its many details. The frothy tulle underskirt reflects the white detailing on the ceiling. On the crisp oversize black-and-white checks of the taffeta cloth is a vase overflowing with green cymbidium orchids—all very pretty against the warm wood paneling.

210. An artfully arranged garland of green cymbidium orchids adds an opulent contrast and masks the support used to drape this gingham top cloth.

211. A tall, slim glass vase draws the eye to this beautiful leaded glass window. Warm-colored branches and leaves complement the upholstered chairs and table linens. Decoration is kept to a minimum, letting the serene, old-world elegance of this lovely restaurant set the mood for an intimate celebration.

212. Position brightly colored flowers near a window to draw the guests' view to a beautiful landscape.

213. If the room has existing urns, add arrangements or branches in watertight plastic buckets or liners that can be slipped into them.

214. Have your florist make a tabletop tree of springtime flowering branches. Hang decorative bags of candy for guests to pluck as they leave the reception.

215. Embellish existing objects in the reception hall. Chandeliers entwined with delicate vines and flowers greatly enhance this room's romantic atmosphere.

216. Potted trees will make a large space look cozier and are available for rent in a variety of types and sizes. Arrange clusters of trees at three different heights in the corners of the reception room or use them to frame the band. Wrap plastic pots with inexpensive fabric to coordinate with the room decor.

217. Keepsake Idea

Fashion a wreath from the same roses and ivy as are used in the bridal bouquet. After the wedding, let the wreath dry to become a keepsake.

218. This gorgeous springtime wreath captures the season with soft shades of green, yellow, white, and blue. The delicate stems of grape hyacinth are clustered together for impact: single stems would get lost among the green and white tulips. A touch of bright yellow adds just the right amount of warmth to the cool colors.

219. If there is a large mirror in the ballroom or in the entrance area, make a gorgeous wreath of colorful flowers or shiny magnolia leaves to frame it. Rather than using a pre-made round wreath form, make a frame from wire to exactly fit the mirror's size and shape.

220. Be sure to decorate the escort-card table with an impressive floral arrangement that will set the tone as guests enter the party: Often something large or tall, or a cluster of small arrangements and candles, will have the right impact.

221. These beautiful champagne spray roses have been paired with garden ivy and offer a warm welcome to guests as they enter the reception venue. This is a perfect example of the beauty of spray roses: Each stem offers blooms that range from fully opened to tiny buds so you can appreciate all phases at once.

222. If you are having a buffet dinner, it is a nice touch to extend the floral decor to the food tables. Keep tall arrangements behind the food and out of the way; or place greenery and low flowers at the table corners and drape a simple garland across the front. Floral decorations should never interfere with the food display.

223

223. Carry out a "green" theme with potted plant arrangements. This urn looks very rustic and casual but you could substitute bright-colored contemporary square pots, aged terra-cotta, or antique silver to coordinate with your style. Choose plants with an interesting mix of leaf sizes, shapes, and colors.

224. The escort-card table is usually the first glimpse guests have of the reception decor. It can showcase an elegant candelabra, feature a large urn bursting with garden roses, or be simply accented with pots of bright green wheat grass.

225. To create an informal garden look use an abundance of flowers with plenty of variety in shape, color, and texture. This low arrangement of roses and lilies has a "just gathered" appeal that suits an outdoor guest book table.

226

Let the centerpieces
reflect your personal style, the season,
or a theme with special meaning.

226. A wine cooler makes a pretty urn for a centerpiece of spring flowers. Perhaps you and your friends are oenophiles and will find the coolers useful after the wedding!

227. Expensive seasonal flowers are often shown to best advantage in sleek, simple containers. These gorgeous red, pink, and white camellias are perfection displayed in a shallow bowl. Just surround with votives and your centerpiece is complete—lots of impact with very little labor!

228. Consider buying your own containers and delivering them to the florist, particularly if you want guests to take the arrangements home after the wedding.

229. Queen Anne's lace adds a delicate, lacy touch to spring and summer floral arrangements. It is available inexpensively, and because it is naturally tall, it is perfect to fill out large arrangements. It is also charming as an accent cascading gracefully over the edge of a small footed urn as pictured in this delightful spring centerpiece.

230. Groupings of small containers make a pleasing change from one large centerpiece in the middle of the table. Just remember to scale the flowers to the containers. Notice how the dainty ranunculus and lilac are perfectly sized to this small cup.

231. KEEPSAKE IDEA

Springtime flowers and grass in tiny silver baskets are not only decorative, if you position one at each place setting they become keepsakes for guests to take home.

232. If the bride and groom are to sit at a sweetheart table that is too small for a centerpiece, ask the florist to substitute lush chair treatments. This garland of roses draped on a gold ballroom chair heightens the romantic look of the table. Scatter small matching rose heads, petals, and votives on the tabletop.

233. Floral arrangements and votives scaled to fit in the center of this small guest table echo the larger flowers and candles on the bridal dais beyond. The pretty roses and miniature carnations are perfectly suited to the small verdigris urns. Beautifully detailed place cards and menu cards enhance the table design.

234. When most of the container will be hidden by the flowers, choose something simple and economical and let the flowers shine.

235. Sparkling table numbers like this one can become part of the centerpiece, eliminating the need for a separate stand to be added to the table.

236. Rustic decorations are more suited to an outdoor setting than to a ballroom. This unusual combination of lady's slipper orchids and chocolate cosmos is successful because it is so beautifully detailed. The graceful use of textures and colors, including bark to cover the cylindrical and cube-shaped containers, contributes to the intriguing design of this table arrangement.

237. If well-designed, small floral arrangements can make a big impact. Fewer flowers mean they must be well-chosen for color and style, and only blooms of impeccable quality and freshness will do.

238. Customize a simple glass vase by lining it with decorative or bi-color leaves to hide the flower stems. Here, the stripes in the leaves pick up the warm tones of the dahlias and roses.

239. For a beach setting, this pretty glass compote was filled with shells in peach tones to match the roses. The glasses and linens pick up the colors of the sea and sky. You could sprinkle white sand in the middle of the table and scatter additional shells to bring the beach right to the guests. You may even be able to find shell votives (shells filled with wax) or pillar candles embedded with small shells to add to the ambience.

240. Create a natural runner by placing large leaves along the center of a rectangular table. The leaves will unify small arrangements and votive candles, creating an area of interest down the table. This is very effective when the tables are too narrow to accommodate larger centerpieces.

241

241. Line a decorative French wire planter with moss for a natural effect. Here flower-filled tin cones hold pretty blooms of anemones, ranunculus, and roses that contrast the soft green moss.

242. Several small silver pedestal dishes overflowing with blooms take the place of one large floral arrangement on this tabletop. Grouped with small glass vases and votives, the centerpieces create a generous display and the multiple pieces provide take-home souvenirs for guests. The strategically placed fruit and flowers add plenty of texture and color to the completed design.

243. If you are renting ornate pedestal dishes, ask your florist to create the arrangements in plastic saucers to sit within the rented containers. Then the flowers can easily be removed at the end of the evening for guests to enjoy at home.

244. Roses, hydrangea, and dahlias, straight from the garden, are accented with an abundance of foliage to make this beautiful centerpiece. Vary the sizes of flowers and leaves to produce an informal garden-style arrangement. Make generous use of foliage to pick up all the green hues in the garden and lawn.

245. Here a cut-glass compote dish is placed atop a glass cake stand to create a tiered arrangement. This is a charming idea for a small at-home wedding, a bridal shower, or luncheon. Just mound small fruits and flower heads to fill the plates. Allow tiny champagne grapes to trail over the edges. The vivid colors pop against the sparkling crystal. Bring out the family heirlooms, like all the crystal serving pieces and the candlesticks with crystal prisms.

246. Be creative and think beyond the container's original use. Fill galvanized watering cans with tulips and daffodils, float single blossoms in wine or brandy glasses, or use a low wooden crate to hold a miniature spring garden. For a French country theme, use tin flower-market buckets with a copper or verdigris finish.

244

247. Silver, crystal, and gilt are always appropriate choices for wedding celebrations. You will find a huge selection of traditional-, formal-, and contemporary-styled floral containers and candleholders to choose from.

248. An assortment of related one-of-a-kind containers, each filled with the same type of flowers arranged to suit its proportions, will give each table a unique centerpiece while creating a harmonious effect overall. If you are not a collector, consult an event planner for sources.

249. Use flared cut-crystal vases to add shape to bouquets. They can be scaled low for dining tables or tall for impact on escort-card tables.

249

250. Set a romantic tone for the dinner by tucking sentimental notes into bright baskets of seasonal flowers placed on each table. This is a sweet idea for a rehearsal dinner too.

251. A three-inch diameter pillar candle nestled into a small floral wreath of open roses and deep burgundy chrysanthemums accented with berries creates a glowing centerpiece for an autumn table. An arrangement combining the flowers and candles takes up less space on a small table—a good choice for a cocktail table.

252. Spring flowers and plants make delightful rehearsal dinner centerpieces. Group several flowering plants with trailing ivy in a basket and tuck in bits of moss to cover the edges of the pots. The baskets could be given to guests as favors or set up the next day on the escort-card table.

253. Contrast flowers and containers to highlight the characteristics of each. Twig baskets, small crates, or even wooden wine boxes make interesting containers for feminine flowers, such as masses of pink roses, tulips, or peonies.

254. Floral foam covered with green moss makes a soft base for velvety red roses. The undulating forms, enhanced by a framework of alternating red votives, create an eye-catching runner down the center of a long table. Neutral linens make a subtle background for the bright colors and strong shapes.

255. Low flowers and candles give an intimate feel to a long table. Guests are able to see and appreciate every bloom and have an unobstructed view to those across the table, making conversation easy.

Flowers for the Reception **175**

256. This formal table centerpiece was constructed on an antique silver stand and features traditional creamy bridal roses, while the graceful cedar foliage, cascading grapes, and pinecones all evoke a fall or winter theme.

257. For drama, choose an interesting centerpiece container like this ornate cast-iron candleholder. It is so striking that it requires only very simple flowers to make a singular statement.

258. Creating arrangements without visible containers is a great way to save money. Plain plastic floral saucers, available in a range of sizes, can be completely covered by flowers and foliage, eliminating the need for a container. Rentals for floral holders such as candelabra, large vases and urns, can add a considerable amount to your floral budget.

To honor your guests and the day,
set the tables with a festive, harmonious
mix of flowers, linens, and tableware.

259

259. This traditionally designed table displays a profusion of romantic deep-pink, open lily blossoms in short fluted crystal vases. The etched crystal stemware and colored water goblets contribute to the lavish atmosphere of the table design. Taper candles in a collection of silver candlesticks add a soft glow.

260. Red goblets provide a beautiful finishing touch to this bright, imaginative table design.

261. Ask your florist or event designer to coordinate all your tabletop decor items with your floral choices.

262. The understated blue-and-white color scheme of this table is enlivened with layered linens and delicate beaded floral embroidery on the topmost cloth. The choice of small flowers, many with tiny blooms on a single stem, include delphinium, hyacinth, snowdrops, stock, and stephanotis. Cream ranunculus with full round heads of soft petals add variety to the floral choices.

263. Start the bride's day with "something blue." Pretty eggcups filled with tiny blue blooms make a beautiful surprise when one decorates each place at a wedding-breakfast table.

264. Ring each plate with a circle of leaves, ferns, or rose petals. If decorating every place setting seems too extravagant or overly time-consuming, just embellish the bride's and groom's place settings at the sweetheart table.

265. This well-coordinated table carries the cheerful pink, yellow, and green color scheme from the flowers to the delicate printed tablecloth and the patterned china and colorful glassware.

266. Pink is a warm inviting color, perfect for a joyous occasion. The deep pinks in this centerpiece are repeated in the rich damask tablecloth and the matte satin napkin, which exactly matches the beautiful open ranunculus. The fresh ivy has been "gilded" with a quick coat of antique-gold craft paint to pick up the gold scrolls in the cloth and add elegance to the floral arrangement. A matching nosegay placed on each napkin adds an extravagant touch.

267. A special napkin will give your place settings a custom look. A classic linen hemstitch napkin is always correct, and lovely monogrammed napkins are available to rent. Try a soft color or a special napkin fold to hold a flower. It is not necessary to incur a great expense for a unique, individual touch.

268. Small, individual details always make guests feel special. An open rose—fresh from the garden—on every napkin continues the floral theme and welcomes each guest.

269. The floral detail on this hand-lettered menu card was chosen to match the soft colors of the linens and flowers.

270. Delicate floral tracery in the tablecloth overlay and napkin trim echoes the floral shapes without overpowering the centerpiece. Although the colors are soft and neutral, the variety of patterns and textures make this table interesting.

271. Colored glasses are a stunning addition to any style decor. Renting them is a splurge that adds an extravagant touch to each place setting.

272. Red pillar candles and a few poinsettias instantly bring holiday flair to this table set with lovely heirloom crystal and china.

273. Demonstrating that silver can be both elegant and contemporary, this table is adorned with lavish but simple rose arrangements that complement the sleek styling of the containers and votives. The absence of greenery enhances the modern look of the design.

273

274

274. Accent a dessert table with a small floral arrangement, like this diminutive white urn filled with a charming collection of coral and yellow tulips, cream and pink ranunculus, and cascading golden-yellow mimosa. The tablecloth and napkins mirror the cheerful shades of the flowers.

275. For a pretty touch, rent colored-glass water goblets to emphasize your flower colors. Use the caterer's standard glasses for wines and champagne and you won't break the budget.

276. Design the decor around a single favorite flower—just use a different color for each table. This is particularly effective with roses because they are available in an endless range of colors. Choose from single-stem or spray-rose varieties to get the perfect shade for each arrangement.

Flowers are a perfect and beautiful choice for wedding cake embellishment.

277. Use the bridesmaids' bouquets to dress the cake table during the reception. Here the base of a simply decorated cake is circled with several bouquets of pastel peonies and white stock. The effect is lovely— and it will make your budget go a bit further.

278. Individual desserts, each topped with a nosegay of flowers, are like personal gifts from the bride and groom, sure to be appreciated by all guests.

279. Brides often have a very clear idea about the perfect wedding cake. Whatever the design, it should reflect the couple's personal style. When planning your cake design, take inspiration from your bridal flowers.

278

280. The traditional all-white cake can be styled with a classic or very modern and sophisticated look. This contemporary cake is a study in textures: The lacy details and the carefully placed three-dimensional roses soften the clean lines of the smooth cake, and add depth and texture.

281. Confectionery flowers can take your breath away when made by a master. Here traditional cymbidium orchids top four pristine pale-pink cake layers. Elegant sugar "pearls" provide a subtle finish to this stylish square cake.

282. Meet with your baker as soon as you have finalized your date and decor style. Popular specialty-cake companies are often booked six months to a year in advance.

Created by Ron Ben-Israel Cakes, weddingcakes.com

283. This delightfully decorated cake boasts a profusion of sugar springtime flowers between each layer—a more extravagant style to be sure, as many flowers are required. The champagne ribbon was matched to a swatch of the bride's dress. Delicate curving stems of lily of the valley and sweet pea add a realistic sense of movement.

284. Instead of rolling the wedding cake into the dining room just before the cutting, display the cake and table as a focal point in the reception decor.

Created by Ron Ben-Israel Cakes, weddingcakes.com

285. Expert Advice:

You are free to choose fresh or sugar flowers to decorate a wedding cake—both are lovely choices. Master cake maker Ron Ben-Israel, of New York City, who created the cakes in photos 281, 283, 287, and 293 says "I like to adorn my wedding cakes with sugar flowers, that way you can have your flowers and eat them too."

286. The rich chocolate frosting on this wedding cake is brightened by a pattern of pale green dots to match the green cymbidium orchids. The chocolate twigs echo the branches used in the tall arrangement on the escort-card table.

287. The gilt details were handcrafted for this magnificent cake topper. The one-of-a-kind "gold" stand holds a dramatic bouquet of red and burgundy confectionery flowers, perfect for a formal winter wedding.

288. A popular trend is to have a collection of small desserts rather than one large wedding cake. Small cakes, tarts, cupcakes, and other desserts can be adorned with flowers and displayed on pretty plates. This cake features cheerful pink roses and traditional ivy on classic white icing.

289. When you choose confectionery flowers to decorate a cake, the range of colors and sizes is unlimited, and there is no need to worry about seasonal availability.

Created by Ron Ben-Israel Cakes, weddingcakes.com

290. KEEPSAKE IDEA

Have your cake topper flowers waxed or a replica made of silk flowers. You can also opt to have only the most delicate accent flowers replaced with fabric flowers. Display the finished keepsake under a glass dome to keep it free of dust.

291. Trim the cake knife to match the floral theme. Ribbons with a few flower buds attached trailing from the knife look very pretty as the cake is cut.

292. Remember to give careful attention to the cake stand and cake table to show off the day's crowning creation. One possibility is to cover the entire top of the table with fresh petals to match the cake flowers.

293. This gorgeous autumn cake features curled fiddlehead ferns nestled among the roses, berries, and miniature vegetables, and a wrap of coppery pleated "ribbon" circles the layers.

294. The crisp, modern look and the bright colors of the fresh-flower details of this cake illustrate how a small cake can make a dramatic statement. The square bottom tier provides a substantial base for the small round tier. The ornate silver stand, scaled to the size of a third cake layer, brings stature to the diminutive design.

295. Have your florist create a miniature replica of the bridal bouquet in fresh flowers to use as a cake topper.

(Opposite) Created by Ron Ben-Israel Cakes, weddingcakes.com

294

~ FIVE ~
MAKING FLORAL DESIGNS AT HOME

This chapter introduces some basic floral design techniques and offers lots of tips to help you create exquisite bouquets and floral arrangements on your own. A wonderful sense of accomplishment and pride comes from creating beautiful items to be enjoyed by others, and if friends or family help you create them, there will be additional pleasure in the endeavor. At the ceremony, wedding guests will marvel at your cleverness.

Simple bouquets, corsages, and boutonnieres are not difficult to make if you master a few techniques to ensure the best results. Centerpieces are very doable once you understand the process. And accessories such as paper cones to hold nosegays or decorated candles are fun and easy. To find the best quality flowers for the best prices, check all available sources: online, local shops, farm markets, and your own garden. Whatever project you consider, make a prototype arrangement and plan carefully so you know exactly how much work needs to be done, how long it will take, and how many flowers you will need. This way, the work will go smoothly for the event itself.

Bouquets, corsages, and boutonnieres you fashion yourself are true expressions of affection.

(297)

296. Beautiful ribbons will add the finishing touch to make your bouquets unique. Satin, taffeta, grosgrain, silk, and organza sheer ribbons in solid colors or stripes, checks, dots, and shaded ombré tones are among the huge selection available to coordinate or contrast with the bridal party's flowers and dresses. Sheer organza ribbon is an excellent choice for personal flowers. If you are misting a corsage or bouquet, water will not spot, stain, or wilt this ribbon, and it will dry looking as good as new.

297. WIRING TECHNIQUES

Flowers and foliage for corsages and boutonnieres must almost always be wired for support. Depending on the flower type and style of the arrangement, it may be necessary to wire flowers for other designs as well. Here are some tips:

- Delicate flowers and foliage should be wired using 28-gauge wire.
- Wire foliage by bending the wire to form a U shape to support the leaf. Use green corsage tape to neatly bind the wire and the stem together, so the wire is not visible.
- Heavier, full flower heads, such as roses and carnations, should be wired by inserting a 6-inch length of wire (longer if the flowers will be used in a bouquet) into the base of the flower head. Pierce the base with a second wire, perpendicular to the first. Bend the second wire and twist all wires together, then bind with corsage tape to make a secure, flexible stem. Use 18-gauge wire for heavy flowers and 22-gauge for smaller flowers.

298. Bouquet in a Foam-Filled Holder

This is a good technique to use when making a bouquet of strong stemmed flowers like roses, hydrangea, or lilac. The soft stems of ranunculus or tulip would snap as you push them into the foam.

Directions

a) Begin with well-conditioned flowers and a bouquet holder that has been soaked in water. It will be easier to work if the holder is secured in a block of Styrofoam or placed in a small heavy vase to keep it stable.

b) Using the largest flowers first, work all around the holder to create a nicely rounded shape.

c) Fill in with smaller flowers, distributing colors and shapes. Add ribbons and short-cut foliage to hide the plastic back of the holder.

d) Pick up the holder and check it all around to make sure the bouquet is full and round, without empty spots.

299. Hand-Tied Bouquet

Hand-tied bouquets can be made a day in advance and placed in a vase of cool water to stay fresh. On the wedding day, dry the stems carefully and wrap with ribbon (see page 208). Hand-tied bouquets can also be displayed in a square or round glass vase to make a long-lasting centerpiece—just omit the ribbon wrap.

Directions

a) Cut flower stems to a comfortable length (about 10 to 12 inches) and remove foliage.

b) Start with a center flower and add stems, turning the bouquet in your hand as you work to spiral the stems around the center flowers.

c) Wrap the bouquet with waterproof green florist's tape to hold the shape, and cut the stems so they are even.

300. Pearl Studded Ribbon Wrap

A hand-tied bouquet can be stylishly finished with a wide, tight wrap of ribbon that is secured with decorative pins. The example shown features pale pink spray roses, opened to the peak of their perfection; it is wrapped with pretty pink ribbon secured with pearl-head pins. To further embellish the bouquet, crisscross a narrow ribbon over the wider ribbon wrap. Letting the stems show gives an informal look. For a formal bouquet, completely wrap the stems from top to bottom.

Directions

a) Create a hand-tied bouquet as explained on page 207.

b) Starting from the bottom, wrap ribbon tightly around the middle section of the taped stems. Work up the stems, covering the end of ribbon as you overlap and wrap toward the top of the stems. When you reach the top, cut the ribbon and turn edge under.

c) Insert decorative pins at intervals to keep the overlapping ribbon in place.

d) Cut the stems evenly below the ribbon.

301. Classic Bow

A multi-loop bow is standard for floral design. Use delicate sheer ribbon for a corsage, rich double-faced satin for a bride's bouquet, and something in character with the design for a wreath. Here are directions for making a five-loop bow; vary the number of loops and the size of the ribbon to make larger or smaller bows.

Directions

a) Hold the end of a length of ribbon between your thumb and first finger. Make a loop and twist the ribbon as you secure it under your thumb. Make more loops, working from each side to the center.

b) The outer loops should be the longest and the center loop should be the smallest. Pinch the center and secure it with floral wire or a chenille stem.

302. Classic Corsages

Choose a single type or several varieties of flowers for corsages; berries or leaves make interesting accents.

Directions

a) Wire several perfect roses and a few accent flowers (see page 205). Bind the wire stems together with corsage tape and cut as needed. Arrange the flowers so no wire shows on the finished corsage.

b) If desired, add a ribbon bow to hide the wired stems or to add fullness between the flowers.

c) Present the corsage with a pearl pin inserted into the stem or attach the corsage to a wrist elastic.

303. Corsages and boutonnieres should be lightly sprayed with water and placed in individual cellophane bags. Tie each bag with narrow ribbon and label it for the appropriate member of the wedding party. Store in a cool place. Keep in mind a home refrigerator can be risky: temperatures that are too cold will ruin flowers.

304. CLASSIC BOUTONNIERE

The traditional rose boutonniere can vary in size, depending on whether you want to use a full open rose, a bud, or a cluster of spray roses. Other flower choices for distinctive boutonnieres are miniature calla lilies and cymbidium and mokara orchids.

Directions

a) Wire the rose (see page 205) and wrap the wire with corsage tape.

b) Back the flower with foliage and tape all the stems together. Cut the stems to be 1 inch to 2 inches long for balance.

c) Refer to the photo for ideas for finishing the boutonniere, for instance: extend one fine wire, wrap with tape, and curl around a pencil; wrap the groom's boutonniere in the ribbon used for the bride's bouquet; or back the flower with a loop made from a narrow leaf.

d) Add a boutonniere pin: a black-headed pin is classic but you might want to use a decorative pin with a colored head.

305. KEEPSAKE IDEA

The easiest way to preserve your bouquet is to dry it. If possible, gently separate the flowers and carefully tie the stems into small bundles. Hang the flowers until thoroughly dried. Flowers should always be hung with the heads down so the stems will dry straight, and with plenty of room to let the air circulate around them. Kept out of bright sunlight, the flowers will last several years.

Fulfill your vision of the perfect wedding decor by making your own centerpieces and accessories.

306. Romantic Canopy

A billowing drape of fabric makes a fairytale setting for an outdoor reception— a perfect spot for romantic wedding photos when the bride and groom pause for their first glass of champagne.

Flowers

- 3 large potted hydrangea plants, weighted at the base
- 6 stems blue hydrangea

Supplies

- 3 poles or sturdy dowels, 7 to 8 feet tall
- 10 yards lightweight white fabric, 50 to 60 inches wide
- Florist's wire or white chenille stems
- 14 to 17 yards blue ribbon, 1½ to 2 inches wide
- 6 green plastic water tubes

Directions

a) Insert the poles into the heavy potted plants (or sink them firmly into the ground, set equidistant apart, as at the points of a triangle). Be sure the poles will not blow over in the wind.

b) Gather up the center of the fabric and wire it to the top of one pole (to be the center of your canopy).

c) Gather the fabric 7 to 8 feet from each end and attach it to the two outer poles, allowing the fabric to drape between poles. Make sure the fabric is well-secured to the top of the poles.

d) Cut the ribbon into 5- to 7-foot lengths and secure to the top of the poles with wire or chenille stems to make flowing streamers.

e) Cut the hydrangea stems and insert them into the water tubes. Wire two tubes to the top of each pole to hide the mechanics of attaching the fabric and ribbons.

307. Basket Arrangement

Beginners will achieve excellent results with this rose-filled rustic basket. Using floral foam makes it very easy to position the flowers exactly as you want them.

Flowers

- 5 STEMS PINK SPRAY ROSES
- 7 STEMS PEACH OR CORAL SPRAY ROSES
- 10 STEMS PEACH HYPERICUM BERRIES

Supplies

- 6-INCH SQUARE BASKET WITH WATERPROOF LINER
- 1 BLOCK FLORAL FOAM

Directions

a) Soak the floral foam and cut it to fit the basket liner and extend at least 1 inch above the basket.

b) Cut the roses and insert stems into the soaked foam. Position some of the flowers low, spilling over the sides of the basket, between the twigs.

c) Add pieces of rose foliage and hypericum berries to fill any spaces where foam is visible.

308. Urn Arrangement

A lovely antique silver dish holds open garden flowers in a romantic loose cascading style.

Flowers

- Eucalyptus foliage
- 3 stems green hydrangea
- 8 open pink peonies
- 3 bunches pink pepper berry
- 6 stems white lilac
- 5 stems blue delphinium
- 3 stems bells of Ireland

Supplies

- ½ block floral foam
- Silver footed bowl or compote, about 6 inches in diameter

Directions

a) Soak the floral foam and secure it to the container with waterproof tape.

b) Insert the eucalyptus foliage low to cascade over the edges of the dish.

c) Add the hydrangea and peonies to create the oval shape.

d) Fill in with pepper berries and lilac.

e) Finish with cut pieces of delphinium and bells of Ireland to add color and enhance the shape.

309. CITRUS-LINED CONTAINER

The container for this arrangement is created by inserting one glass cube vase inside another, slightly larger one, and filling the gap between them with lemon slices. You could use leaves or berries instead of lemons.

Flowers

- 3 CORAL PEONIES
- 3 PURPLE ALLIUM
- 12 STEMS ROSES (THREE EACH OF PINK, CORAL, ORANGE, AND YELLOW)
- 6 STEMS LAVENDER
- 3 STEMS BUPLEURUM
- 2 STEMS YELLOW KANGAROO PAWS

Supplies

- 2 SQUARE GLASS VASES: ONE 5 INCHES, ONE 3 OR 4 INCHES
- 6 LEMONS, SLICED

Directions

a) Place the smaller square vase inside the larger one and use a dull knife to push the lemon slices into the space between them. Fill the small vase with water.

b) Gather the flowers into a loose hand-tied bouquet and cut the stems to fit the interior vase.

310. Fern Candles

Candles decorated with ferns or other plant material add a pretty touch to a naturalistic wedding decor.

Ferns

> A few stems of assorted ferns: asparagus, leather leaf, or maidenhair

Supplies

- Ivory pillar candles, 2 inches and 3 inches in diameter
- Matte-finish decoupage or acrylic medium (both available at craft or art supply stores)
- Soft paintbrush

Directions

a) Hold the fern in place on a candle and brush gently with the decoupage medium. It will seal the fern in place.

b) For a more colorful look, apply pressed blue and lavender hydrangea florets to the candles in the same manner. (To press flowers and petals, lay them between sheets of waxed paper and place in a thick book until flat and completely dry.)

311. Fresh-Flower Cake Topper

To top a wedding cake with fresh flowers, make an arrangement in a small floral foam holder and insert it into the cake. One good design option is a miniature replica of the bridal bouquet. Small nosegays or individual flowers can be placed directly into the icing. Thoroughly wash and dry all flowers and foliage before decorating the cake, and after cutting the cake, remove them before serving.

Flowers

- 5 OPEN MEDIUM-SIZED ROSES
- 4 ROSEBUDS
- 12 TINY SPRAY ROSES
- A FEW CLUSTERS OF BERRIES

Supplies

- SMALL FLORAL FOAM HOLDER (ALSO KNOWN AS AN "IGLOO")

Directions

a) Arrange the flowers in the floral foam so the completed piece will sit on the cake without any space visible at the bottom or between the flowers.

b) If you wish, using additional flowers, make clusters of one or two roses with a few buds and berries to place on layers.

312. Floating Daffodils

The pretty cup-shaped heads of daffodils float well and the green candles are colorful companions in this very simple centerpiece. Daffodils are usually not seen cut this short, but are a great choice for a spring celebration; they also are very affordable and open quickly. Roses, dahlias, and many other flowers would work equally well.

Flowers

- 8 TO 10 STEMS OPEN DAFFODILS

Supplies

- 2 GLASS BOWLS, 12 INCHES AND 8 INCHES IN DIAMETER
- 8 DISC-SHAPED FLOATING CANDLES, 2 INCHES IN DIAMETER

Directions

a) Center the smaller bowl in the larger one and pour a small amount of water into each.

b) Add the candles to the center bowl.

c) Cut the stems from the daffodils and place the flower heads in the large bowl to encircle the bowl of candles. Adjust water levels as needed.

313. CONES

It's easy to make paper cones to hold small nosegays, favors, or tossing petals. Use decorative papers in colors to match your wedding theme.

Directions

a) Enlarge the pattern at left below. Trace it onto the decorative paper and cut it out.

b) The top left corner of the pattern is the top of the cone. Roll the shape. Secure with double-stick tape, staples, or a dab of hot glue.

c) Trim with a ribbon bow or decorate with a seal of the couple's initial.

d) If using to hold tossing petals, fill the cones and stand upright in a basket, ready to be offered to guests.

e) If you will be hanging the cone, punch 2 holes as indicated and thread with a narrow ribbon.

(a)   (e)

PHOTOGRAPHY CREDITS

Numbers indicate the page on which a photo appears.

Azzura Photography: 116

Courtesy of Ron Ben-Israel Cakes, www.weddingcakes.com: 193, 194, 196, 200

Pierre Chanteau: 166

Susie Cushner: 107

Christopher Drake: 43

Richard Felber: 44 right, 147

Robert Gattullo: 13, 21 bottom, 22, 23, 28, 34, 46 left, 59, 60, 63, 64, 71, 78, 79, 82 bottom, 83, 84, 85, 86, 87, 88, 90, 95 right, 101 (both photos), 104 bottom, 105, 108, 109, 158 left, 172, 173, 174, 183, 202, 205, 206-207, 209 (both photos), 210-211, 214

Getty Images: James Baigrie: 33, 148; John Blais: 188; Jessica Boone: 175; Augustus Butera: 187; Jennifer Cheung: 163; Dana Gallagher: 2-3, 4, 80; Lisa Hubbard: 154; Richard Jung: 70, 143; Ray Kachatorian: 192; Walter B Mackenzie: 95 left, 104 top; Alison Miksch: 132, 216; Ngoc Minh Ngo: 40; Jeremy Samuelson: 58, 114, 215; Solaris: 128, 142; Sozaijiten/Datacraft: 161; Julie Toy: 102; Michael Weschler: 178

Thomas Hooper: 35 left

iStockphoto: 14, 36 top, 66 right, 97 top, 120, 125, 144, 146, 150, 152, 164, 195, 219; Urmas Aaro: 27; Tatyana Aleksandrova: 126; Rebecca Child: 21; Gheorghe Cosoveanu: 66 left; Alessandro Drago: 157; David Freund: 199; Konstantin Goldberg: 136; Melissa Jill Hester: 119; Scott Leman: 99; Shaun Lowe: 76, 208; Andrew Manley: 201, 218; Gordana Serreck: 122 right; Sarah Thomas: 124; Lisa Thornberg: 20 top, 100; Merijn van der Vliet: 130

Robert Kent: 5 second from bottom, 35 right, 36 bottom, 39, 50, 53, 139, 140, 177

Charles Maraia: 18 left; 68 top, 74, 145 (both photos)

Jeff McNamara: 5 top and bottom, 11, 26, 32, 54, 55, 81, 159, 169, 220

Susan McWhinney: 111, 191

William Meppem: 69, 112, 121

David Montgomery: 41

Courtesy of Original Runner Company, www.originalrunners.com/973-744-7070: 117 (both photos)

Toshi Otsuki: 6, 8, 12, 15, 16 (both photos), 17, 18 right, 20 bottom, 30, 37, 47, 48, 56, 57, 82 top, 89, 91 left, 92, 94, 96 left, 97 bottom, 98, 110, 129, 134, 135, 158 right, 165, 168, 170 right, 180, 186 bottom, 190, 204, 212

Luciana Pampalone: 5 second from the top, 10, 61, 68 bottom, 176, 186 top, 189

David Prince: 9, 38, 42, 45, 72-73, 75, 91 right, 96 right, 106, 115, 151, 170 left, 198, 217

Steven Randazzo: 171, 197

Maurice Rougement: 51

Wendi Schneider: 160

Leyla Sharabi: 67, 122 left, 123, 131, 155, 179

Michael Skott: 167

Walter Smalling: 103

Carlos Spaventa: 93

Joe Standart: 19, 29, 31, 49, 52, 62, 127, 153, 184

William Steele: 65, 138

Ann Stratton: 137, 185 (both photos)

Tim Street Porter: 149

Courtesy of Victoria magazine: 162

Dominique Vorillon: 25, 141, 156

Mindy Wass: 44 left, 181

Elizabeth Zeschin: 182

INDEX

Note: Page references in *italics* indicate specific design projects.

A

Accents
    berries, 61, 64, 92–93, 95, 104, 173, *214, 215, 216, 218*
    chocolates and cookies, 74–75
    ferns in ice or candles, 72–73, *217*
    herbs, 64–65
    unusual, 62–73
Aisles
    bouquets for, 120–125
    outdoor weddings, 118–120, 122
    personalized runners for, 116–117
    petals for, 118, 126–127
Arches and arbors, 128–131
Autumn flowers, 20–21

B

Banister decor, 141
Baskets of flowers, 44–45, 106–107, *214*
Berries. *See* Accents
Blue flowers, 42–45, 85
Bouquets, 79–99
    for attendants, 97–99
    bows for, *209*
    colors. *See* Colors of flowers
    cone holders for, 115, 121, 122, 166, 167, *220*
    construction methods, 81, *205*
    design projects, *204–211*
    foam holders for, 81, *206*
    hand-tied, 12–13, 38–39, 59, 78, 79, 81, 88, 92, 124, *207, 208*
    jewels dressing up, 88
    keepsake ideas, 85, 91, 95, 96, 151, 211
    long, cascading, 82, 83
    long-lasting, 79–81
    mixing colors and textures, 95
    nosegays, 35, 53, 64, 88, 89, 90, 98, 102, 109, 122
    for petite brides, 92
    pomanders, 108, 109, 125
    ribbons for. *See* Ribbon(s)
    roses in, 78–79, 81–85, 88–99
    shape of flowers creating, 35
    for tossing, 96
    tussie mussie holders for, 66, 102–103
    wired, 81, *205*
    wiring techniques, *205*
Boutonnieres, 21, 65, 77, 104–105, 209, 210–211
Branches, seasonal, 21
Bridesmaid's bouquets, 97–99, 109, 190, 191

C

Cake flowers, 190–201
Candles
    for beach setting, 165
    centerpieces and, 165, 173, 177
    Christmas weddings and, 138–139, 186
    with ferns, 72–73, *217*
    floating daffodils and, *219*
    low flowers and, 174–175
    pink and red flowers with, 47, 53
    uses for, 20, 113, 140
Canopy, making, *212–213*
Centerpieces, 156–177
    for beach setting, 165
    candles in, 173, 177
    candles in lieu of, 165
    chair garland instead of, 160
    containers for, 156, 157, 164, 168–171, 174
    design projects, *214–217*
    roses in, 161, 164–167, 168, 172–177
    rustic, 162, 163
    small groupings/small spaces and, 159–161, 162, 167
    table numbers in, 162
Ceremony flowers. *See also* Aisles
    about: overview of, 113
    arches and arbors, 128–131
    canopy, *212–213*
    vestibule area, 114–115
Chair covers, 129, 130, 144
Chocolates and cookies, 74–75
Christmas (winter) weddings, 22–25, 138–139, 186
Colors of flowers
    accents enhancing. *See* Accents
    blues, 42–45, 85
    contrasting with container, 32, 41
    contrasts and combinations, 34–37
    depth and visual interest with, 35
    dramatic mixes, 68, 69
    greens, 58–59
    mixing textures with, 95
    pinks, 46–49
    reds, 50–53
    single-color, 30–31
    strong combinations, 32
    suggesting country garden, 34
    unexpected mix of, 60–61
    whites, 54–57
    yellows and oranges, 38–41
Cone holders, 115, 121, 122, 166, 167, *220*
Corsages, 77, 101–102, *205,* 209–210
Crowns, 86

D

Design projects
    about: overview of, 203
    bouquets, corsages, boutonnieres, *204–211*
    bows, *209*
    centerpieces, *214–217*
    cones, *220*
    floating daffodils, *219*
    flower cake topper, *218*
    romantic canopy, *212–213*

F

Fathers, boutonnieres for, 77, 105, *211*
Fern candles, 72–73, *217*
Floating flowers, 54, 55, 168, *219*
Flower girl, flowers/accessories for, 44–45, 106–111
Fragrant/nonfragrant flowers, 31, 32
Fruit with flowers, 64

G

Garden flowers, 12, 14, 16–19, 36, 155
Green flowers, 58–59
"Green" theme, 154
Grooms, boutonnieres for, 65, 77, 104–105, 211

H

Halo, 108, 109
Headpieces, 77, 86–87, 98, 108, 109
Herbs, 64–65

K

Keepsake ideas, 71, 85, 91, 95, 96, 151, 159, 198, 211

L

Lavender, 61, 66

M

Meanings of flowers, 71
Menu cards, 161, 185
Mothers, flowers for, 66, 77, 101, 102, 105

N

Nonfragrant flowers, 32

P

Personal flowers, 77. See also Wedding party flowers
Petals, for aisle and tossing, 118, 126–127
Pink flowers, 46–49
Purple/blue flowers, 42–45, 85

R

Reception flowers. See also Centerpieces; Table settings
about: overview of, 133
on buffet food tables, 152
chair covers matching, 144
chandeliers and, 137, 138, 139, 149
for Christmas weddings, 138–139
complementing window views, 146, 147
creating welcoming ambience, 134–137, 140

on escort-card table, 27, 152, 155, 173
fabric and linens complementing, 136, 137, 142–145
"green" theme, 154, 155
as guest keepsakes, 159, 167
informal garden look, 155
linen selection and, 143
opulent, formal weddings, 134–137
potted trees and, 149
roses, 152–153, 155, 186–187, 189
rustic inn setting, 137, 140
tabletop tree with candy bags, 148, 149
tall, slim vases for, 143, 146
wreaths, 150–151
Ribbon(s)
colors and types, 97, 205
pearl studded wrap, 208
streamers, 84, 85, 96, 109
Roses
best look for, 28, 29
for bouquets, 120–122, 124
bouquets with, 78–79, 81–85, 88–99
boutonnieres, 104
on cake, 192, 193, 196, 197, 200, 201
in centerpieces, 161, 164–167, 168, 172–177
Christmas-themed, 23
contrasting with container, 32, 41
garland for chairs, 160
headpieces, 86–87, 98, 108, 109
meaning of, 71
open, on every napkin, 184
petals for aisle and tossing, 118, 127
as reception decor, 152–153, 155, 186–187, 189
red, 50–53
romantic tradition of, 19
shades of same color, 32–33, 38
single-color bouquets, 30–31
single-stemmed, 49
softly colored, 49
spray, 49, 214
strong color combinations, 32
unexpected mix of flowers with, 61

wreaths with, 150–151
year-round availability, 28

S

Seasonal branches, 21
Seasonal flowers
autumn, 20–21
spring, 9–13
summer, 14–19
winter, 22–25
year-round availability, 9, 26–29
Silk flowers, 86, 87, 108, 109, 110, 125, 198
Spring flowers, 9–13
Summer flowers, 14–19

T

Table settings, 178–189
coordinated presentations, 178–189
menu cards, 161, 185
single-flower, 68
small arrangements or tiny vases, 68, 159, 181
vibrant unusual flower mix, 70, 71

W

Waxed flower keepsakes, 91, 96, 198
Wedding cake flowers, 190–201
Wedding party flowers
about: personal flowers, 77
bouquets for. See Bouquets
for brides. See Bouquets, Headpieces
for bridesmaids, 97–99, 109, 191
corsages and boutonnieres, 100–105, 209–211
for fathers, 77, 105, 211
for flower girls, 44–45, 106–111
for grooms, 65, 77, 104–105, 311
for mothers, 66, 77, 101, 102, 105
White flowers, 54–57
Winter flowers, 22–25
Wreaths, 24, 95, 113, 138, 150–151

Y

Yellow flowers, 38–41

Editor: Carol Spier
Book Design and Illustrations: Jon Chaiet
Photography Editor: Martha Corcoran

Library of Congress Cataloging-in-Publication Data
Wagner, Diane.
  Beautiful wedding flowers : more than 300 corsages, bouquets and centerpieces / Diane Wagner.
     p. cm.
  "Victoria."
  Includes index.
  ISBN 978-1-58816-798-9
  1. Flower arrangement--Handbooks, manuals, etc. 2. Wedding decorations--Handbooks, manuals, etc. 3. Bridal bouquets--Handbooks, manuals, etc. I. Title.
  SB449.5.W4W34 2010
  745.92'6--dc22
                            2010007150

10 9 8 7 6 5 4 3 2 1

Published by Hearst Books
A division of Sterling Publishing Co., Inc.
387 Park Avenue South, New York, NY 10016

Victoria is a registered trademark of
Hearst Communications, Inc.

For information about custom editions, special sales, premium and corporate purchases, please contact Sterling Special Sales Department at 800-805-5489 or specialsales@sterlingpublishing.com.

Distributed in Canada by Sterling Publishing
c/o Canadian Manda Group, 165 Dufferin Street
Toronto, Ontario, Canada M6K 3H6

Distributed in Australia by Capricorn Link (Australia)
Pty. Ltd.
P.O. Box 704, Windsor, NSW 2756 Australia

Manufactured in China

Sterling ISBN 978-1-58816-798-9